WILLING WORDS

Time
distilling poetry,
is time, when
I'm refining and defining
Me

WILLING WORDS

An Ode to Poetry

SHARRON GREEN

Author Photo: Hattie Stewart-Darling @hattie_darling
Cover and other photos: Sharron Green

You can find Sharron Green on social media:
Instagram, Facebook, Threads, X & TikTok: @rhymes_n_roses

Website: https://rhymesnroses.com

Independently published in 2024.

Author's Note

Willing Words is a collection of poems about the process of writing, finding inspiration and the satisfaction of completing a poem. Amongst other themes it champions the use of poetry forms and rhyming; examines the physical discomfort of writer's block and explores the force that compels poets to poetize. In sum, it is my ode to poetry, and features versions of various forms including the elfchen; golden shovel; rhupunt; sestina; sonnet; than-bauk and zejel.

I'm pleased to say that a few of these pieces have already appeared elsewhere, and I am grateful to those involved in their selection. They are: The Words that Turned, shortlisted for the Arts Richmond Roger McGough Poetry Prize 2023 and included in the *Turning Point* anthology; Many a True Word in *Finding our Voices Write out Loud Woking—the first six years*; Where the Truth Lies in Episode 13 of Kathleen McPhilemy's Poetry Worth Hearing and My Dream Poem shared by BBCUpload on National Poetry Day 2023. In addition, My Poetry Style and Chants for Nature are also in my first pamphlet, *Introducing Rhymes_n_Roses*.

Thank you for reading. I'd be very grateful for a review and to know your thoughts as a reader or writer of poetry. Plus, if you have enjoyed Willing Words please take a look at my other publications.

Sharron

@rhymes_n_roses

Sharron Green © Photography

Contents

Sharron Green © Photography

Many a True Word

Never trust a poet,
they are wearing a disguise,
you might think they are listening
but they are plotting lies.

Like magpies they are spying gems
that others haven't spotted,
just watch and they will swipe them
and soon they'll be re-potted.

You'll think—where did that come from?
It sounds so fresh and new!
But someone else inspired it,
it could even be you!

So never trust a poet
they are at least two-faced,
though their work is eco friendly
as no word goes to waste.

To Please, Prickle

My rhymes attempt,
sometimes unkempt,
supine and bent
to tease, tickle.

Their forms can sway,
through storms they may
break norms, foray,
like fleas – fickle.

They ooze with ease,
like booze from bees,
post snooze or sneeze,
to please – prickle.

Dovetails

Porcelain plumage peels from the page,
surging in steep, undulating waves.

Tattooed with our thoughts, dreams, wishes –
our essence, soaring through skies,
your passage our presence.

Pure, vital energy, powers your flight,
a conduit of conscience, a ciphered insight.

The chorus of cooing enchants every ear,
singing our scribbles and channeling cheer.

Our duty's to set down words worth
your endeavour,

as etched in the ether they will live forever.

Dawn and Dusk

Dawn and dusk are sacred times,
creating drama for our rhymes.

Perched on the cusp of day or night,
words will tumble into sight.

Unfettered by the human gaze,
that's drawn to marvel at the blaze.

On the page the thoughts will fuse,
bathed in pink and orange hues.

They speak of wonder, thanks and praise,
for past, present and future days.

And so the skies display a portal
from the living to immortal.

The Words That Turned

Scrambling through the synapses
of scattered cerebral cells.

Contorted into tunnels, warrens, burrows –
borrowed and self-hewn.

Shunting rivals from the pendulous nib,
sacrificial siblings shorn.

Hunting rituals, meditative then manic,
panic as hunger haunts.

Dancing, beguiling, seducing serpentine
semantics, 'til slaked and sated.

Spitting, snarling, savage, turning
timid, tempered, tame.

Free-falling from the heavens,
descending to the shimmering page.

Swooping to secure tenancy,
spear salvation, restore symmetry.

Nature's call to come together,
meld and mate, create poetry.

Poeting

I like spotting
your jotting down,
plotting rhyme frown.

Thick brows knitting,
not quitting just
sitting non-plussed.

Try relaxing,
face facts 'n know—
that's how thoughts flow.

Confessions of a Poet's Lover

Oh no, she has that look again,
tapping away like she's insane,
dear Lord spare me from the pain,
of another ruddy rhyme!

She gazes out for inspiration,
you'd think a marvellous creation,
was about to grace the nation –
what a waste of time!

At first I used to make a joke,
conjure a friendly jibe and poke,
I'm not a poem-loving bloke,
it's not my cup of tea.

But that just seemed to make her sad,
or worse, go crotchety and mad,
and maybe, some are not that bad,
after a pint or three.

Sharron Green

Spanish Lullaby

at this hour silence rings
peels of peace like ivy clings
cloaked in fleecy angel's wings

time to put myself to bed
rest my bones, reset my head
but I'm on my phone instead
scrolling, tapping things

need to drag myself away
but this poem has its way
wants to be let out today
before the first bird sings

so this is my first zejel
it's not great but what the hell!
they're informal – can you tell?
how my tiredness stings

Shall I Read You?

Shall I read you?
Will your words skip from the page
and tantalise my tongue?
Twist and turn and tumble out in torrents
or trickle timorously?

Shall I read you?
Will I process your emotions and intent?
Place myself within
your tortured exuberance?
Empathise with your screams?

Shall I read you?
Will my heart beat to your rhythm
and vibrate with your vitality?
My lungs swell with the weight of your dreams
and propel them to the ears of angels?

Shall I read you?

Poetic Pox or Paean

What if poetry were an illness,
and its dispersal was deplored?
And with every rhyme released
the mortality rate soared.

What if it were a craving,
too strong to be ignored?
And our cognitive awareness
mixed up riveted with bored.

What if we rhyming poets suddenly
saw our work as flawed?
And desperately deleted all the
words set down and stored.

What a tragic situation,
one the world can ill afford.

So, let's carry on creating,
armed with pen as sword.

For one day soon our brilliance
will be lauded and adored,
(if not at least our drug of choice
has not yet been outlawed).

My Poetry Style

Poetry's pretty, poetry's quick,
sometimes it slips off the tongue, it's so slick.
Poetry's old, the ancients would use it,
it helped to recall things—but now we abuse it.
Back in the days when they had much more time,
people got pleasure from hearing a rhyme.
Were they more simple, and easily pleased?
Or did yesterday's poets also get teased?

Many great works, now recited and treasured,
were written in verse that was carefully measured.
Some prefer rhyming and I'm one of those.
At the moment it's less of a challenge than prose.
It can be contrived, but for me it's a sport,
to turn into tune, a genuine thought.
Others would choose a more natural style,
it's maybe more honest and lacking in guile.
It sticks to the point and can be more grand,
there's less risk of sounding too woolly and bland.

Since starting to write, I've done some research,
and found that today, poetry's a broad church.
Some write for pleasure, and others to preach,
some find it healing—a bit like a leech.
It seems there are lots of ways to get printed,
but no likelihood of ending up minted.
I think I'll continue to develop my style,
combining nostalgia with raising a smile.

My Quarry

I ink for thought,
I mind for gold,
I nudge at nuggets,
paint them bold.

The well is deep,
the echo clear,
some words spring out
some lurk in fear.

Then on the page
sleek doodles loop
connect with blots –
poetic soup.

Chants for Nature

Could words weave nature's beauty
with requisite eloquence?
Is their uniform unequal
to a challenge so immense?

The iridescent colours,
the geometric splices,
the intricate complexity,
outshine our dull devices.

When the task's too monumental,
why do we even try,
to eulogise a sunset
or a rainbow in the sky?

Our words will always fail to paint
a picture that is real,
but alluding to all senses
may convey the way we feel.

And enable all to visualise,
internalise, be thrilled,
so once immortalised in ink,
that pleasure's deep instilled.

Where the Truth Lies

"Let yourself be the '*you*' you want to be.
The path to true peace is a stranger to lies.
If you follow me, you too will be free,
floating on cotton clouds up in the skies.
Hurl away habits and nudge off all norms –
abstract is true art so fling off all forms!"

> *"You'll be at sea if you cast away forms.*
> *Bobbing about is just how you will be.*
> *Lack of constriction is where chaos lies.*
> *In verse, as in life nowt good can be free.*
> *The song of a sonnet soars to the skies,*
> *there can be no shame in following norms."*

"No shame, maybe, but my brain numbs with norms.
Frankly, my dear, there is no fun in forms.
Disastrous duty is all it can be.
Alliteration is littered with lies.
Refrains restrain – you will never be free.
Meter so measured just sullies the skies."

> *"Sorry, I'm sick of this slush about skies.*
> *Civilisation is centred on norms.*
> *We'd all be mush if we didn't have forms.*
> *Poetry helps us define how to be,*
> *yes, with some licence, we have scope for lies,*
> *but structures, like ladders can set us free."*

"Chill out! Don't freak out! My opinion's free –
you cannot curtail my reach for the skies,
but if you insist on sticking to norms
you may spend your life completing those forms.
Pity personified is what you'll be,
the inverse of happy, drowning in lies."

> *"Let's bury this tiff, this way no peace lies.*
> *If we've time to rhyme, we are truly free.*
> *There's room for all poets under the skies.*
> *Deeply devoted to challenging norms,*
> *there's truth in our words with or without forms.*
> *Even though, we 'know not what we may be'.*

So, let's follow forms or else ignore norms.
Creativity lies in open skies.
Set yourself free, be what you want to be.

Drunken Syllables

Drunken syllables splash my page,
perverting passive rhyme to rage.
Tempered tone twists towards torrid.
Wholesome humour hateful, horrid.
Resulting rant makes my eyes mist.
Resolve – never to post when pissed.

Willing Words

Pulled into a poem
like pork stretched from the bone,
I tiptoed from my writing
to be snapped, back in the zone.

Searching for a prompt,
a place to rest some words,
cluttering my head
those whirls of swirling birds.

Released onto the page
they jostle into line,
a game of consequences
clinging to a spine.

Quizzically I survey
the mass that they have clustered,
hoping it will tempt
their mates to cut the mustard.

Sharron Green

T o m o r r o w

Tomorrow I will write a p o e m
to help tackle today. To t o u c h
upon the e x p o s e d nerves with
words I cannot say. Tomorrow's
poem will be short, within s a f e
walls confined. A padded cell of
sanity—an escape from my mind.

Writer's Block

It's hard to write when there's a block.
You stare in space or watch the clock.
It's easier when there's no theme,
you have a wander, change of scene,
just write a bit to get you going—
save it for later, never knowing
if later it will have a use
or if it's let the juices loose,
creative ones, I mean, of course
there shouldn't be a need for force.
Then suddenly your writing's back
and you resume familiar track,
but fear lurks, when you take your pen,
Will I be stuck for words again?

Alone Together

alone together
your tail I trace
nose to the floor
a looping pace

through frozen ferns
your feather quills
pricked by the air
graffiti spills

we smile the skies
tune into birds
devour views
and suckle words

and in the peace
a poem sorts
alone together
inking thoughts.

My Dream Poem

I've woken up this morning with a smile upon
my face,
the kind that happens when my mind is in
a happy place.
You see last night I wrote a rhyme that really was
a star—
I hesitate to claim it but it was my best
by far.
It was quite philosophical with truths that
tumbled free –
the key to save the world was there and all
in poetry.
I'd posted it on Insta and it had a great
reception
many had enjoyed it and admired my deep
perception.
At forty lines it made a dent in homework that
is due –
I knew I'd never reach that if I dabbled with
haiku.
So now I drift awake to find my dream piece was
just that,
I don't know what to do now coz I can't hand in
this tat!
One day we will awake to find our dreams have been
recorded,
I'm hoping mine are killer rhymes and not something
too sordid!

Modern Rhymes

Poetry needs honesty,
poetry needs pain.
If you're too shy or proud to share
your poems may be
lame.

You need to grab attention,
stir empathy or pity.
It helps if your words can convey,
how life is often
shitty.

It's best to have a point of view,
be bold and cause offence.
No need to follow any rules,
or even make much
sense.

There's little scope for rhymers
as the fashion is for prose,
though wit can overcome this
as Brian Bilston
knows.

These modern times
prescribe, sometimes,
new voices and new themes,
a rejigging of world order,
a mining of fresh seams.

I'm trying to get the measure of
the landscape before me,
it's not known if my comfort zone
can stretch far,
but we'll see.

Trudging Lanes

Chasing Pavements by Adele,
love the song, but truth to tell,
had to Google what that means,
now I know—it's chasing dreams.
Armed with hope but doomed to fail –
searching for a holy grail.

Chasing sounds too energetic –
I just plod, it's less frenetic.
Pavements are so hard and grey,
thicker soles make them OK.
Shall I give up? No, I'll be fine,
trudging lanes and tracing rhyme.

Reflections on Rejections

How many times must I submit
before I've nothing left to share?
and all my entrails have been strewn
whilst judges pick and trawl and tear.

How can I make my subjects fit
conform to rules that are not there?
Will all I write be out of tune
with truths I'm unequipped to bare?

How do I know when I should quit,
accept that life just isn't fair?
Will this drag on or finish soon?
Will I be sad or just not care?

Why do I strive to win a prize
for work that's priceless in my eyes?

Sharron Green

Unread Pages

unread pages
sit forlorn
feeling wasted
words unborn
gently open
lay them bare
allow locked lungs
alchemic air
consume contents
save and share

Taking the Plunge

~After Don Marquis

Have a punt at	publishing
imbibe the rush that it can bring,	a
pride of plume in each	volume
uncensored, unrestrained	of
voice, your choice, your purse, your	verse
your fizz, your whizz, your being	is
embedded in each word you write, there's nothing	like
the spike, the popping, true jaw-	dropping
reeling feeling, heartbeat-stealing when	a
book blooms like a	rose
each word a crafted	petal
of the kind you can't put	down
you gently cradle, stroke	the
pages, picture prizes, premiering in the	Grand
then build an oeuvre, craft a canon, fill a	Canyon
fuelled by flames of fans	and
feed their fevered	waiting
never sating their desire	for
more as through	the
ages your words	e c h o

'Publishing a volume of verse is like dropping a rose petal down the Grand Canyon and waiting for the echo.'

McCollum (ed.) (1982) *Selected Letters of Don Marquis*. Northwood Press.

Sharron Green

Time Will Tell

My orchard's full of low hung fruit.
The blushing harvest holds my gaze.
Autumnal verse in proud parade.

Odes to Halloween rip ripen.
Christmas crackers bide their time.
The Spring, a twinkling haiku, buds.

But what holds back? What won't unfurl?
What shy concoction waits for light?
There's something half-formed, all unsaid.

I smile at it, it's reticent.
Soft petals cup raw sentiments.
Respectfully, I pick the ready rhymes.

Why I Write

I'm doing this for me, for you,
for me it is a pleasure.
I write these lines in quiet times,
I write them at my leisure.

Sometimes I want to say something,
sometimes I need ideas.
I often find when walking,
my poetry appears.

It creeps up through the bracken,
it hides in wildflowers.
I tickle it from synapses,
as rainbows shine through showers.

The words occur in order –
or spill out in a tumble.
I try to catch them on my phone,
but later it's just mumble.

I'm doing this for me, for you,
but maybe more for me,
I really hope you like it, though
I guess I will soon see.

Sharron Green © Photography

Acknowledgements

Firstly thanks to Kevin and Sam for giving me the time and supporting the results of my musings, and to Dougie the Dog for waiting patiently whilst I jot them down on walks.

A special thank-you to Sarah Drury and Reena Doss for helping me to edit, design and publish *Willing Words*.

Thanks to my fellow Booming Lovelies, Heather Moulson and Trisha Broomfield, plus Heather Cook, Karen Izod and Victoria D'Cruz, my early readers. Also Carla Scarano D'Antonio whose enthusiasm and creativity we miss.

I'd like also to mention Pam Ayres and Brian Bilston, wonderful poets who have raised the profile and recognise the enduring popularity of rhyming poetry.

As always, I'd like to show my appreciation for the international Instagram poetry community for their inventiveness & inspiration. Particularly the following accounts, some of which prompted the poems shared here:

@altpoetryprompts
@a.j.butlerwriting
@coralynn.poetry
@darakalima
@fawnpress
@gwensaintmary
@helenography
@inkgladiatorspress
@inksomnia_poetry

@lindalokheeauthor
@lrsterlingpoetry
@meh_poets
@miriamo77
@randomerbobsxyz
@swellversed
@thesealeychallenge
@truculentbutamiable
@t.z_writer

Sharron Green © Photography

Early praise for Willing Words

Willing Words is a lyrical tour-de-force: an ingenious approach to redefining the trials and triumphs of being a poet. Sharron's immaculately crafted rhyme combines great insight, elegant imagery, and masterly use of poetic form and structure. *Sarah Drury*

A classy collection that will inspire poets and readers everywhere. With just the right level of poignancy and humour and a profound subtext. I really like the variety of structures too. Well done. Love it. *Heather Moulson*

I can't tell you how much I've enjoyed looking through this clever and immensely entertaining collection! It should be available on prescription for aspiring poets, or poor old poets who are at the end of their tether trying to get a poem out of their heads and down on paper. There were a number of lines which made me feel like punching the air, shouting, 'Sharron's expressed beautifully what I've been mumbling about for years!' *Heather Cook*

Don't underestimate the rhymes in this book, Sharron's words are insightful, incisive, inspired and on occasion, in your face. Underpinning this wonderful collection is an infectious sense of fun. *Trisha Broomfield*

Willing Words has a gentle humour, at times funny, at times resonant of Pam Ayres. It is also an exposition of what can be conveyed through rhyme and a full use of poetic form. *Karen Izod*

An astounding collection of poetry to inspire poets and aspiring writers by someone who unashamedly champions rhyme and poetic form. Sharron is a cross between Brian Bilston, Pam Ayres and Wendy Cope. Witty rhymes, deep thinking, sharp observations all served up with a warm yet wry smile. *Victoria D'Cruz*

Hattie Stewart-Darling © Photography

About the Author

Sharron Green loves roses and rhyming poetry. Her acclaimed work seamlessly blends modern life, nature and nostalgia, gaining her a strong and loyal following on social media—where she's better known as Rhymes_n_Roses.

As a confident and skilled performance poet, Sharron is also the host of two open mic poetry nights in South East England; Solar Sisters in Guildford and Write out Loud Woking. She also performed at the Guildford Fringe Festival as part of the trio of poets called The Booming Lovelies.

Sharron's work has been published in over 15 international anthologies. She also has two other chapbooks—*Introducing Rhymes_n_Roses* and *Viral Odes* (the latter published by Ink Gladiators Press).

In 2022, she graduated with an MA in Creative Writing from the University of Surrey and was a head writer for the Surrey New Writers Festival in 2023. Sharron lives with her husband and golden retriever Dougie in Guildford, near London in the U.K.

Instagram, Facebook, Threads, X & TikTok: @rhymes_n_roses
Website: https://rhymesnroses.com

...on the page
sleek doodles loop
connect with blots –
poetic soup...